Pyramids

Pyramids
Structurally Based Tasks for ESL Learners

Student's Book

Carolyn G. Madden and
Susan M. Reinhart

Ann Arbor   The University of Michigan Press

To David and Marcus
To José

Copyright © by The University of Michigan 1987
All rights reserved
ISBN 0-472-08073-3
Library of Congress Catalog Card No. 86-51231
Published in the United States of America by
The University of Michigan Press
Manufactured in the United States of America

1990   4   3

Line illustrations by Betsy James

Photograph of Austin, Texas, courtesy of the
   Austin Convention and Visitor's Council

Photograph of party courtesy of Moya Brennan

Photographs of Eastern Michigan University
   dormitory room and campus courtesy of
   the Office of Information Services and
   Publications, Eastern Michigan University

Composite photograph of the solar system
   courtesy of the National Aeronautics and
   Space Administration

Photograph of New York City courtesy of the
   New York Convention and Visitors Bureau

Photograph of Philadelphia courtesy of the
   Philadelphia Convention and Visitors Bureau

Photographs of student, wedding gown, classroom, and
   street © José Sánchez H., 1986. All rights reserved.

Photograph of the University of Miami campus
   courtesy of the University of Miami

Photographs of university dormitory room,
   Ann Arbor, and Michigan League
   courtesy of the University of Michigan
   News and Information Services

Acknowledgments

We gratefully acknowledge the help of our colleagues and students at the University of Michigan who participated in the field-testing of the manuscript.

We would also like to thank Larry Selinker for his encouragement during the initial stages of the project, Virginia Samuda for sharing her knowledge of task-based learning with us, John Swales for offering helpful suggestions for improving the manuscript, and Terry Madden and Ele McKenna for their support of the project.

We would like to thank the following people for helping us make the tapes for *Pyramids:* James Bixler, Mary Fairman, Sally Fairman, Ahmed Ferhadi, Roderick Fraser, Steven Guice, John Haugen, Tomoko Tamura, Betsy Soden, and John Swales.

To the Teacher

Pyramids is designed for low and low-intermediate students who have had some exposure to English. The primary goal of the book is to provide students an opportunity to build on and strengthen their repertoire of grammatical structures through the use of task-based activities. Students work together in pairs or in small groups on such legitimate "chores" of everyday communicative life as describing people, comparing cities, evaluating universities, and stating opinions. Each task features particular language points that are usually highlighted in summary exercises.

The tasks offer a range of input to the student, i.e., listening, reading, and using visual and shared information. Students use this input as a way of getting new information and as a guide and context for using particular structures. Then the exchange of information takes place through question asking and answering or discussion. Finally, students synthesize the information to solve a problem, express an opinion, summarize, or make a decision. As they carry out and accomplish these tasks, students are called upon to actualize their own awareness of structures, pool their resources, and assimilate the language of their environment. The summary exercise (or exercises) in each lesson offers students an opportunity to practice and focus on the accurate use of a particular structure.

Pyramids can be used both in the United States and abroad, although a few of the lessons are geared toward students who want to study in the United States. The book is appropriate for students in intensive courses and can be used with reading and writing materials related to the general topics of the lessons or with grammar books, for additional language practice. The book is also excellent for nonintensive adult education students, providing integrated and challenging tasks that reflect the language activities of their everyday world.

Pyramids contains a student's book with twenty-four lessons, a teacher's book, and tapes. The lessons include several integrated language structures listed in the table of contents and in the teacher's book.

To the Teacher

The teacher's book includes general comments on classroom management; a section that provides a comprehensive description of the language covered in each lesson, a list of materials and suggested procedures for classroom management of each lesson, and an answer key; and tape scripts.

Two tapes accompany the text, since some listening activities involve the use of divided information. One group of students is asked to extract information from Tape A and the other group from Tape B. For teachers who have only one tape recorder or no tape recorder at all, the teacher's book offers alternative procedures for teaching these lessons.

Pyramids, through various inputs, exchanges, and discussions, provides students an opportunity to communicate and to generate the necessary language for completion of tasks. *Pyramids* is a task-based textbook providing students with integrated use and practice of grammatical structures in meaningful contexts.

Contents

Lesson 1   **New Students**   1

Main Language Focus: requesting and giving personal information, simple present tense (verb *be*), statements and questions

Other Language: occupations, countries, hobbies and interests, dates, spelling

Lesson 2   **Stick Figures**   4

Main Language Focus: describing people, descriptive adjectives, simple present tense (verbs *be*, *have*), statements and questions

Other Language: facial features

Lesson 3   **Who Was at the Party?**   6

Main Language Focus: describing people, descriptive adjectives, simple present tense (verbs *be*, *have*, *work*), statements and questions

Other Language: occupations

Lesson 4   **Lost and Found**   8

Main Language Focus: describing objects and articles of clothing; simple present tense (verbs *be*, *have*); statements, questions, and negatives

Other Language: expressions of time and place; vocabulary for shapes, clothing, and material; spelling names; expressions *What's it like?*, *What does it look like?*

Lesson 5   **What Doesn't Belong?**   12

Main Language Focus: simple present tense, statements and negatives

Other Language: *it*, *can't*, names of common objects

Lesson 6 **Trip to Bermuda** 14

Main Language Focus: describing, simple present tense (verbs *have, cost*), *there is/there are*, statements and negatives

Other Language: scanning for specific information, hotel vocabulary and symbols

Lesson 7 **The Unfinished Picture** 20

Main Language Focus: describing, simple present tense, *there is/there are*, statements and negatives

Other Language: restaurant vocabulary, prepositions, expression *is missing*

Lesson 8 **Compatible Roommates** 24

Main Language Focus: getting and giving information about habits and routines; making comparisons; simple present tense; comparative forms (*both, neither, too, either, but, and*); statements, questions, and negatives

Other Language: likes and dislikes, interests

Lesson 9 **Furnishing a Dorm Room** 30

Main Language Focus: discussing the location of objects, prepositions of place

Other Language: colors, furniture and objects commonly found in a dorm room, giving and getting suggestions

Lesson 10 **The Living Rooms** 34

Main Language Focus: describing where things are located; prepositions of place; *there is/there are;* statements, questions, and negatives

Other Language: furniture, objects commonly found in the home

Lesson 11 **Is There a World of Difference?** 38

Main Language Focus: describing educational systems; present tense; quantifiers (*some, few, most, all*) and adverbs of frequency (*always, generally, rarely, hardly ever*); statements, questions, and negatives

Other Language: school vocabulary, past tense

Lesson 12 **First Day in the United States** 42

Main Language Focus: narrating; simple past tense; statements, questions, and negatives

Other Language: scanning for specific information, *ago, nobody*

Lesson 13 **Alibi** 48

Main Language Focus: simple past tense; statements, questions, and negatives

Other Language: scanning schedules and ads for specific information, drawing conclusions

Lesson 14 **How Good Is Your Geography?** 52

Main Language Focus: superlatives, geographical terms

Other Language: comparatives

Lesson 15 **Choosing a City** 60

Main Language Focus: describing and comparing; comparative and superlative forms; statements, questions, and negatives

Other Language: *there is/there are*, present tense (verbs *be, have*)

Lesson 16 **Apartments for Rent** 65

Main Language Focus: describing and comparing; comparative and superlative forms; statements, questions, and negatives

Other Language: apartment vocabulary

Lesson 17 **Advertisements** 69

Main Language Focus: *too* and *enough*

Other Language: scanning advertisements

Lesson 18 **The English Language Academy** 72

Main Language Focus: *too, too much, too many, enough*

Other Language: clarifying problems and making suggestions; count and noncount nouns; present tense; statements, questions, and negatives; school vocabulary

Lesson 19 Exploring the Universe 76

Main Language Focus: comparing, superlatives and comparatives

Other Language: numbers, vocabulary relating to solar system, talking about the future, *will, is/are, going to, may, might*

Lesson 20 Choosing a University 82

Main Language Focus: comparing; comparative forms; simple present tense; statements, questions, and negatives

Other Language: scanning for specific information, making choices, helpful information about choosing an American university

Lesson 21 Traffic Laws 87

Main Language Focus: modals: *can, can't, must, mustn't, have to, don't have to, should, shouldn't*

Other Language: traffic expressions and signs, explaining rules, offering opinions, quantifiers (*most of, all of, some of, a few of, none of*)

Lesson 22 Planning a Weekend 92

Main Language Focus: modals: *should, could, have to, would rather ('d rather)*; making suggestions and choices; giving opinions

Other Language: entertainment vocabulary

Lesson 23 Hiring an E.S.L. Teacher 98

Main Language Focus: present perfect, describing job experience and education

Other Language: making comparisons, *ago, for*

Lesson 24 Questionnaire 103

Main Language Focus: present perfect; statements, questions, and negatives

Other Language: modals: *can, will*

Lesson 1 — New Students

▣ Here are some information cards for four new students in Level 2 at the English Language Academy. Some information is missing from them. Listen to the conversation and write in the missing information about the new students.

Name: _Gabriela_
Country: _Portugal_
Birth date: _8/25/50_
Married ☑
Single ☐
Occupation: _doctor_
Interests and hobbies:
reading & photography

Name: _Samuel_
Country: _____
Birth date: _2/4/65_
Married ☐
Single ☐
Occupation: _student_
Interests and hobbies:
classical music

Name: _Kuniko_
Country: _Japan_
Birth date: _____
Married ☐
Single ☐
Occupation: _____
Interests and hobbies:
volleyball & swimming

Name: _____
Country: _Morocco_
Birth date: _____
Married ☐
Single ☐
Occupation: _____
Interests and hobbies:
_____

1

Lesson 1

Complete the following summary about Kuniko:

Kuniko is _____ Japan. She was born on _____. She _____ married. She _____ Japanese. She is a student and she _____ to play volleyball and swim.

- Now find out the same information about some of your classmates by interviewing each other. Complete an information card for each classmate you interview.

Name: _____
Country: _____
Birth date: _____
Married ☐
Single ☐
Occupation: _____
Interests and hobbies:
_____

Name: _____
Country: _____
Birth date: _____
Married ☐
Single ☐
Occupation: _____
Interests and hobbies:
_____

Name: _____
Country: _____
Birth date: _____
Married ☐
Single ☐
Occupation: _____
Interests and hobbies:
_____

Name: _____	Name: _____	Name: _____
Country: _____	Country: _____	Country: _____
Birth date: _____	Birth date: _____	Birth date: _____
Married ☐	Married ☐	Married ☐
Single ☐	Single ☐	Single ☐
Occupation: _____	Occupation: _____	Occupation: _____
Interests and hobbies: _____	Interests and hobbies: _____	Interests and hobbies: _____

- Review the information about your classmates and complete the following paragraph about one of them.

_____ is from _____ . _____ birth date is _____ . S/he is _____ . S/he speaks _____ . S/he is a _____ and s/he likes to _____ .

Now write about another classmate or about yourself.

_____
_____
_____
_____

Student Notes:

Lesson 2   Stick Figures

- Create a stick figure, using ideas from the drawings provided. Then, describe your stick figure to your partner.

Listen to your partner's description. Then, draw his/her stick figure here. *Do not look at your partner's picture.*

Your stick figure:

Your partner's stick figure:

Lesson 2

happy    sad    mad    tall   short   medium height

skinny    thin    average weight    heavy    pregnant

curly hair    straight hair    wavy hair    bald

short hair    medium length hair    long hair

a beard    a moustache    freckles    big eyes    glasses

Lesson 3 Who Was at the Party?

📼 Helen went to a party last night. She is talking to her friend Kelly. Kelly wants to know who was at the party. Listen to the conversation and fill in the chart with as much information as you hear about the following people. *Not all the squares will contain information.*

	Linda	Robert	Paul	Clara
Occupation	*engineering student*			
Height				
Weight				
Hair				
Other				

Lesson 3 7

- Read the following descriptions of the people at the party. Correct any mistakes. One correction has already been made.

    Linda was at the party. She has long brown hair and wears glasses. She is tall and heavy. She's an ~~English~~ *engineering* student.

    Robert and Paul were at the party too. They both study at the library. Robert isn't cute and has a beard. He's medium built. Paul is shorter than Robert. He speaks with a New York accent. People like him—he's terrible.

    Clara also went to the party. She's tall and unattractive. She has straight, dark brown hair. She works at the art museum.

- Write about some of the students in your class. Include two mistakes for each student. Share your descriptions with other class members and have them correct your mistakes.

    _____
    _____
    _____
    _____
    _____
    _____

Student Notes:

Lesson 4   Lost and Found

- With your partner, find and discuss the differences in each set of articles. *There are two differences per set.*

1.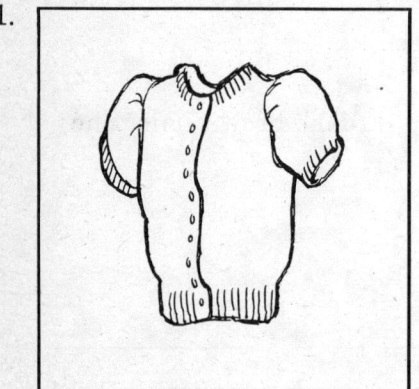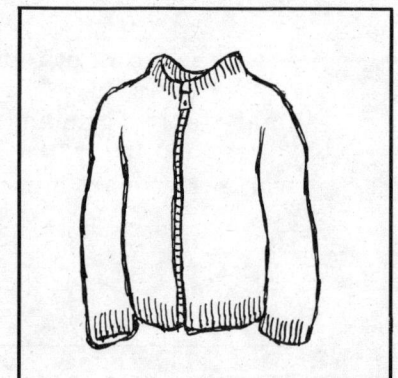

2.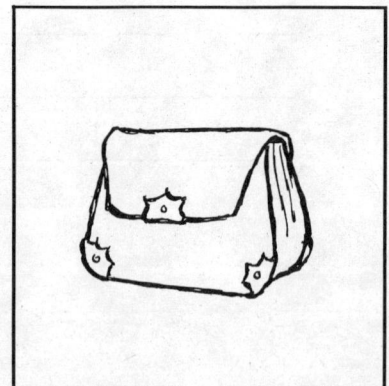

3.

 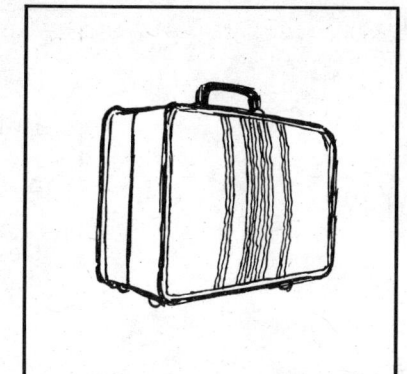

4.

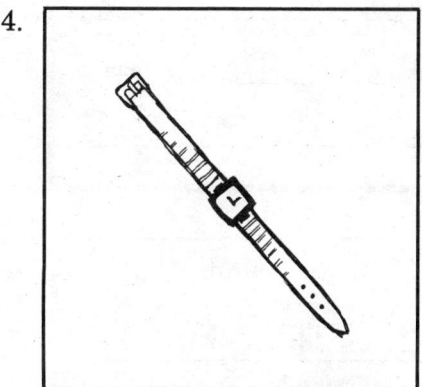 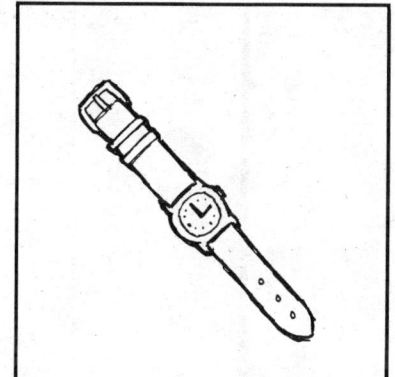

5.

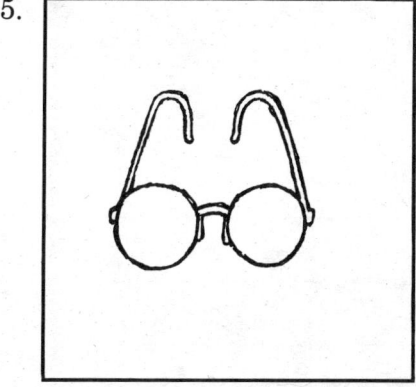 

Lesson 4

📼 Three people have lost articles at their college. They call the college Lost and Found to inquire about the articles they have lost.

1. Listen to the conversations and fill in a Lost and Found form for each conversation.

2. Check your answers with other students in your class.

Lost and Found

Date: _March 14_

Article: _watch_

Description of lost article:

Name: _____

Date lost: _Mar. 14_   (a.m.) / p.m.

Place: _____

Student Notes:

Lost and Found

Date: _March 14_

Article: _____

Description of lost article:

Name: _____

Date lost: _____   a.m. / p.m.

Place: _____

Lost and Found

Date: _March 14_

Article: _____

Description of lost article:

Name: _____

Date lost: _____   a.m. / p.m.

Place: _____

Lesson 4 11

- Write a Lost and Found report that describes each of the articles shown in these drawings.

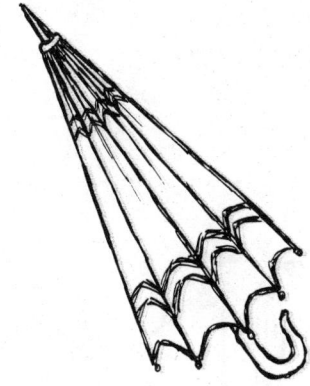

Lost and Found Report

Date:

Article:

Description:

Lost and Found Report

Date:

Article:

Description:

Lesson 5   What Doesn't Belong?

- With your partners, look at the groups of objects in boxes A through K. Decide which object doesn't belong in each box and explain why. Then draw a group of objects in box L.

Lesson 5 13

- After your group has finished talking about the pictures, write down what doesn't belong in each box and why. The first answer has already been filled in.

A. *The fork—because it isn't a fruit.*
B. _____
C. _____
D. _____
E. _____
F. _____
G. _____
H. _____
I. _____
J. _____
K. _____
L. _____

Student Notes:

Lesson 6   Trip to Bermuda

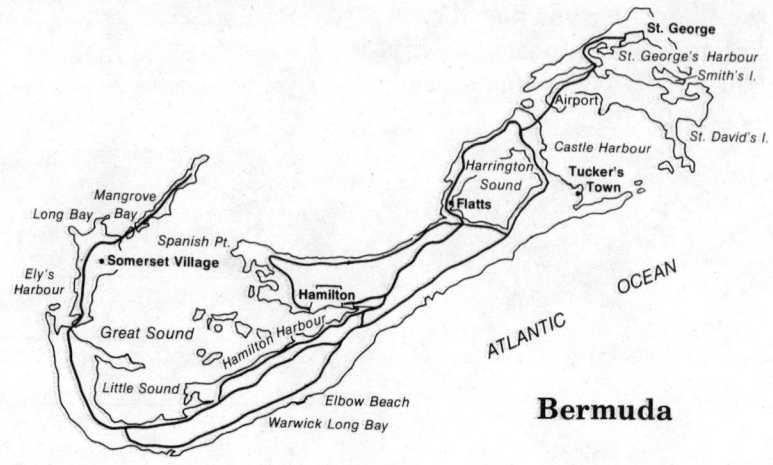

🔊 Carla is going to take a vacation to Bermuda. She calls a travel agent to find out information about how much it will cost. Listen to the conversation and write down the missing information in the box provided.

Name: _Carla Morgan_

Address: _425 Second St._

Tel. no.: _479-1651_

Credit card: —

Hotel: _____

    price for single room: _____

    price for double room: _____

    meals included:

        _____ all meals

        _____ 2 meals

        _____ Continental breakfast

Transportation to hotel: _____

Available at hotel:

    _____ pool

    _____ tennis

    _____ sauna

    _____ golf

    _____ beach

    _____ cocktail lounge

    _____ entertainment

Flight information:

    airline: _____

    prices: _____

    _____

    tax: _____

Lesson 6   15

- What is the approximate cost of transportation within Bermuda? Read the following paragraph and write down the information in the space provided.

TRANSPORTATION—Perhaps the most common and economical means of transportation in Bermuda is cycling. Motor-assisted cycles may be rented for about $15 to $23 a day; safety helmets are required. For the hardier visitor bicycles are available for about $5 to $7 a day. Cycle rental operations are found throughout the island and at many of the large hotels. Roads in Bermuda are narrow, hilly, curving and banked in many spots by coral walls. Due to a law forbidding the use of automobiles by nonresidents, car-rental services are not available. Carriages with fringed tops may be hired for $7.50 per half hour for two persons. Taxi fare from the airport to Hamilton is about $13–$14. Regular bus service throughout the islands is provided; the one-way fare from the central bus terminal on Washington Street in Hamilton to St. George's or Somerset is $2, from Hamilton to the aquarium in Smith's Parish about $1. Passenger ferries link the city of Hamilton to Ireland Island, Somerset and Watford Bridges, and Paget and Warwick Parishes. The trip to Somerset takes an hour and costs $2 each way.*

Transportation	Available?	Costs
Bus	_____	_____
Cycles	_____	_____
Train	_____	_____
Rental cars	_____	_____
Bicycles	_____	_____
Other: _____		_____

*Reprinted, by permission, from *Travel Guide to the Caribbean: Bahamas, Bermuda and Other Ports of Call* (Falls Church, Va.: American Automobile Association, 1986), p. 45. © AAA—reproduced by permission.

Lesson 6

- Here is some information on the cruises Carla is interested in taking when she arrives in Bermuda. Using this information and the other information you have already gathered, fill in Carla's expenses. What will be the approximate cost of her trip to Bermuda?

Alibi Dream Sail*

All day or half day sailing trips on 'Alibi'. Enjoy a swim in a delightful cove and a refreshing complimentary rum swizzle, beer, or soft drink. Trips leave from Albuoy's Point Wednesdays and Fridays. $35.00 per person including lunch for all day trips. $17.50 per person for half day trips. Departure times are 10:00 a.m. and 2:00 p.m. Tuesday, Thursday and Saturdays for the half day trips. Phone 8-0774.

Bermuda Island Cruise: *

Bring your bathing suit and towel and cruise aboard a luxury motor yacht on an exciting informative 5½ hour water tour to Treasure Bay for a Bar-b-que lunch, swimming or basking in the sun. An afternoon trip to Somerset Village and a leisurely stroll to Mangrove Bay. Calypso entertainment and swizzle party on board. $30.00 per person and $23.00 each senior citizens (age 65 years and over). Leaves Albuoy's Point, Hamilton at 11:00 a.m. returns 4:30 p.m. daily except Sunday. Phone 2-8652.

Glass Bottom Boat Cruise:*

Bermuda's hidden wonderland of coral, plants and undersea life opens up before your eyes on this 2-hour cruise to Bermuda's Sea Gardens on Bermuda's largest glass bottom boat. Sit back in comfort and enjoy the lively commentary by the Bermudian captain. Leaves from the Ferry Terminal, Hamilton at 10:00 a.m. and 2:00 p.m. daily except Sunday. $14.00 per person. Phone 2-8652

Carla's Expenses	Costs
Hotel (Thursday, Friday, Saturday, Sunday, and Monday nights):	$ _____
Airfare:	$ _____
Transportation to and from hotel:	$ _____
Food (lunch and dinner are about $25/day):	$ _____
Cycle rental:	$ _____
Tours:	
Alibi Dream Sail (half day)	$ _____
Glass Bottom Boat Cruise	$ _____
Total:	$ _____

*Reprinted, by permission, from *This Week in Bermuda* 40, no. 9 (March, 1986): 24.

Lesson 6

- Look at the following hotel symbols. What do you think they mean?

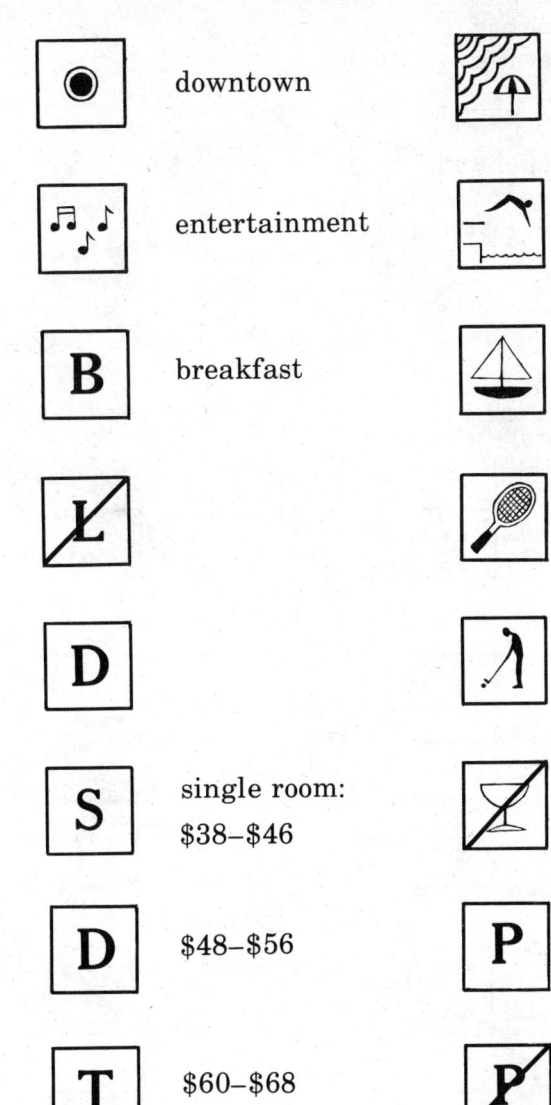

downtown

entertainment

breakfast

D

single room: $38–$46

$48–$56

$60–$68

Lesson 6

- You and your partner are planning to go on vacation to Bermuda. You have information about two hotels there, the Harbor Hotel and the Sand Hotel. Discuss the information and then together decide which hotel you like better.

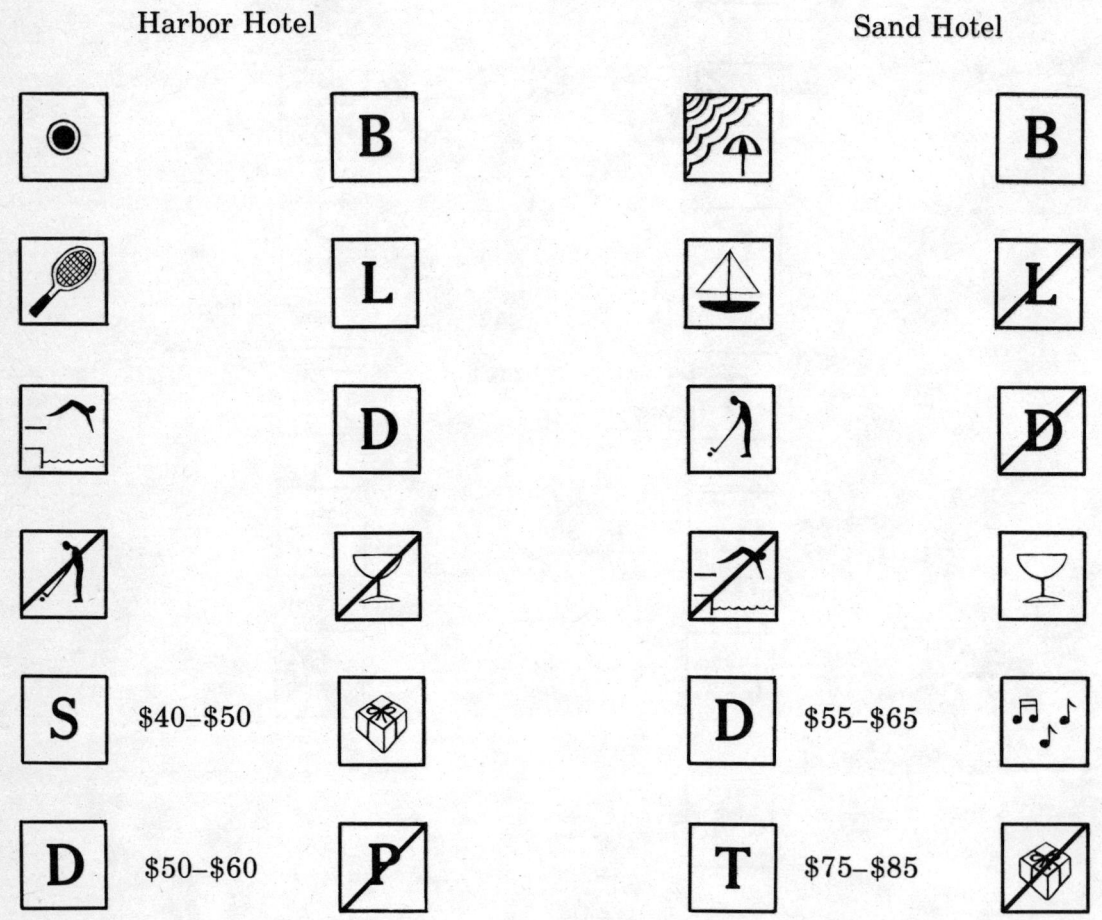

Lesson 6   19

Recommend the hotel to a friend by telling your friend in a letter why you chose this hotel.

March 12, 19 ____

Dear _____ ,

I've decided to stay in the _____ Hotel in Bermuda. It's a good hotel near _____ . It has _____ and _____ _____ . There's no _____ , but _____

_____

_____

_____

_____

Best Wishes,

Student Notes:

Lesson 7   The Unfinished Picture

- What's funny about the picture on page 21? What is missing? How many things can you find? Write them down.

1. _____
2. _____
3. _____
4. _____
5. _____
6. _____
7. _____
8. _____
9. _____
10. _____
11. _____
12. _____

Lesson 7   21

- This Restaurant Questionnaire was prepared by a group of E.S.L. students. Use the questions to find out about your classmates' restaurant customs. Write down the information on the questionnaire. Then, discuss the differences you find.

Restaurant Questionnaire

In your city or country:	Classmate's Name:	Classmate's Name:	Classmate's Name:
1. What time do restaurants usually open and close for dinner?			
2. How do you get the waiter's attention at a restaurant?			
3. Do waiters and waitresses have to speak a foreign language to work in a restaurant?			
4. If you don't like the food at a restaurant, do you say something?			
5. Do most restaurants serve liquor or have a bar?			
6. What percent do you usually tip in a restaurant?			
7. What happens if you don't have enough money to pay the bill?			
8. How often do you go to a restaurant to eat?			

- Write a description of your favorite restaurant.

_____

_____

_____

_____

_____

_____

Student Notes:

Lesson 8   Compatible Roommates

📼 A housing officer is interviewing two women who are looking for a roommate for the dormitory.

1. Listen to the interview and write down the answers to the interviewer's questions on the questionnaire. The teacher will assign half the class to Tape A (Paula) and the other half to Tape B (Roseann).

2. When you have written down the information from your tape, check your answers with the other students in your group.

3. Exchange information with a partner from the other group and write down the information on the questionnaire. *Do not look at your partner's paper.*

Student Roommate Questionnaire I	Paula	Roseann
1. Age?		
2. Smoke?		
3. Get up?		
4. Go to bed?		
5. Stereo or TV?		
6. Loud music?		
7. Musical instrument?		
8. Sports?		
9. Weekends?		
10. Study: how many hours?		
11. Talk a lot?		
12. Neat or messy?		
13. Clean: how often?		

Lesson 8

- Would Paula and Roseann make compatible roommates? Compare them and then fill in the blanks with a word or phrase.

1. Neither of ___them___ smokes.
2. Roseann gets up early, and Paula does _____.
3. Both of them _____ a TV, and Roseann _____ a stereo, too.
4. Paula _____ on Saturday night, but Roseann doesn't.
5. _____ play musical instruments. Roseann _____ the guitar, and Paula _____.
6. Roseann likes loud music, but Paula _____.
7. Roseann likes to swim, and Paula _____ too.
8. _____ of them is neat. Paula is messy, and Roseann _____.
9. Roseann doesn't _____ a lot, and _____ doesn't either.
10. _____ Roseann _____ Paula clean once a week.

- As roommates, Paula and Roseann seem fairly compatible. Name *two* ways you think they are *incompatible*.

1. _____
   _____
2. _____
   _____

Student Notes:

- In the interview, what questions did the housing officer ask to find out about the following? One question has already been filled in.

1. Age: _____ *How old are you* _____?
2. Smoke: _____?
3. Get up: _____?
4. Go to bed: _____?
5. Stereo or TV: _____?
6. Loud music: _____?
7. Musical instrument: _____?
8. Sports: _____?
9. Weekends: _____?
10. Study (how many hours): _____?
11. Talk a lot: _____?
12. Neat or messy: _____?
13. Clean (how often): _____?

What other questions would you ask?

14. _____?
15. _____?
16. _____?
17. _____?

Lesson 8

- Fill in the Student Roommate Questionnaire II with information about yourself. Then interview your partner to find out the same information and complete the questionnaire.

Student Roommate Questionnaire II	You	Your Partner
1. Age?		
2. Smoke?		
3. Get up?		
4. Go to bed?		
5. Stereo or TV?		
6. Loud music?		
7. Musical instrument?		
8. Sports?		
9. Weekends?		
10. Study: how many hours?		
11. Talk a lot?		
12. Neat or messy?		
13. Clean: how often?		

Lesson 8 29

- How are you and your partner similar or different? Would you make compatible roommates? Why or why not? Write a short paragraph that answers these questions. Then discuss your conclusions with the class.

  _____

  _____

  _____

  _____

  _____

  _____

Student Notes:

© José Sánchez H., 1986

Lesson 9   Furnishing a Dorm Room

- You and your roommate want to furnish your dorm room.

1. From the drawings, pick out what you and your roommate want to put in your room. Then decide where you will put each item. For example, where do you want to put the beds? What about the desk? And the map? Draw a picture of each item, or write its name, on the floor plan.

2. By the way, the room needs painting. Choose a color.

3. When you have finished, show the floor plan of your furnished room to the other people in the class. Discuss how the rooms are different.

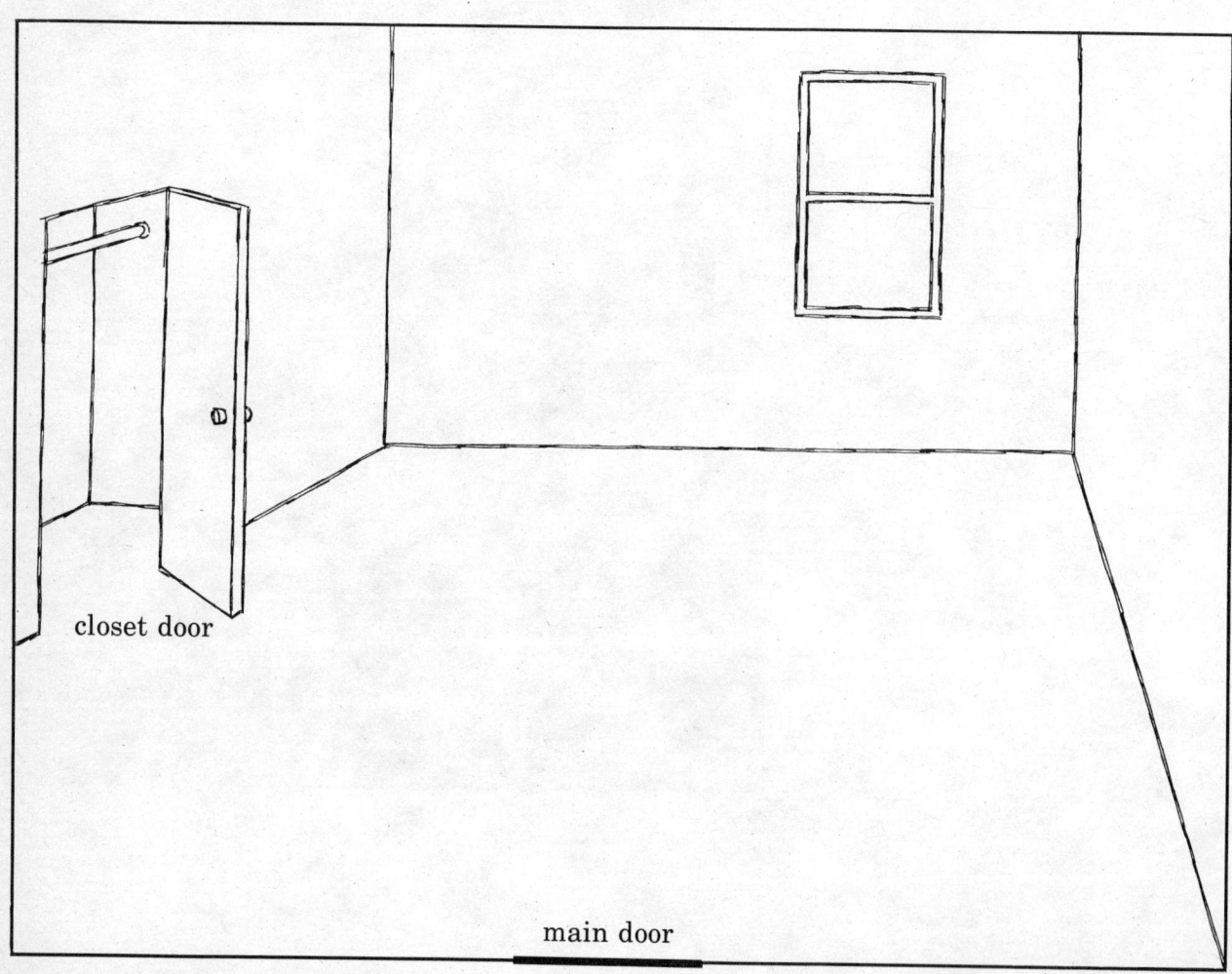

Floor Plan

Furnishings

Lesson 9

 or

1 or 2   1 or 2

 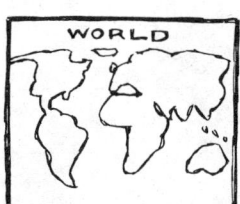  

1 or 2   1 or 2

    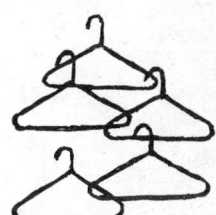

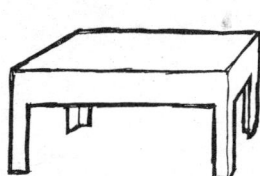  

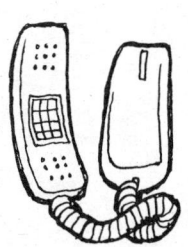  

yellow?
white?
beige?
green?
blue?
pink?
??

Lesson 9

- After you and your partner have finished talking about your dorm room, complete the following sentences:

1. The map is _____.
2. The chair is _____.
3. The wastepaper basket is _____.
4. The magazines are _____.
5. The ceiling lamp is _____.
6. The hangers are _____.
7. The dresser is _____.
8. The flowers are _____.

Give short answers to these questions:

1. Is the calendar over the desk? _____.
2. Are the flowers on the bookcase? _____.
3. Is the desk in the center of the room? _____.
4. Are the beds next to each other? _____.

Student Notes:

Lesson 10   The Living Rooms

- You have been assigned to living room *A*. Look at the picture and describe your living room to your partner.

Find the differences between your living room and your partner's living room. *There are eight differences.*

Lesson 10 35

- After you and your partner have found the differences, write them down.

1. *In my partner's living room* _____
   _____
2. _____
3. _____
4. _____
5. _____
6. _____
7. _____
8. _____

Student Notes:

- You have been assigned to living room *B*. Look at the picture and describe your living room to your partner. Find the differences between your living room and your partner's living room. *There are eight differences.*

- After you and your partner have found the differences, write them down.

1. *In my partner's living room*
2.
3.
4.
5.
6.
7.
8.

Student Notes:

Lesson 11   Is There a World of Difference?

▣ A teacher is giving a lecture to his English class on the educational system in the United States. Listen to the lecture and take notes if you wish.

Notes:

Now, answer the following statements by circling **T** if the statement is true, **F** if it is false. If the statement is false (**F**), change the word in italics to make the statement true. Check the answers with your partners or the teacher.

Student Notes:

1. *Some* children go to private school in the United States.   T F

2. Children *always* go to elementary school for 6 years.   T F

3. Children are *generally* required to attend school until they are 16.   T F

4. Boys and girls *rarely* go to school together.   T F

5. *Few* schools teach math and science.   T F

6. A foreign language is *hardly ever* required in college.   T F

- The teacher is willing to answer questions about the educational system in the United States. Prepare and write down questions about the following topics and find out the answers from your teacher or other students in the class.

1. Uniforms: _____?

2. Grades: _____?

3. Hours per day: _____?

4. Requirements for college: _____?

5. Summer vacation: _____?

Do you have any other questions?

6. _____?

7. _____?

- Work in small groups. Discuss the following generalizations and take notes about how your countries differ from or agree with the statement. When you have completed the activity, share your findings with the rest of the class. What are some of the major differences among your educational systems?

1. Children start school at five years old.

   your country: _____

   other countries: _____

   _____

2. Most children go to public school.

   your country: _____

   other countries: _____

   _____

3. All children study art, music, and sports in elementary school.

   your country: _____

   other countries: _____

   _____

   _____

4. Children do not wear uniforms to school.

   your country: _____

   other countries: _____

   _____

5. Teenagers choose some of their own courses in high school.

   your country: _____

   other countries: _____

   _____

6. Students do not have to take a foreign language in high school unless they plan to go to college.

   your country: _____

   other countries: _____

   _____

7. Students must be 16 before they are allowed to leave school.

   your country: _____

   other countries: _____

   _____

8. School vacation begins sometime in June and ends the first week of September.

   your country: _____

   other countries: _____

   _____

9. Smoking is only permitted in colleges and universities, not in high school.

   your country: _____

   other countries: _____

   _____

10. Boys and girls study together.

    your country: _____

    other countries: _____

    _____

- Write a short history of your educational experience. Include information about when you began school, your class size, your favorite teacher, subjects you studied, etc.

_____
_____
_____
_____
_____
_____
_____
_____
_____
_____

Lesson 12 — First Day in the United States

📼 A foreign student is talking to another student about her first day in the United States. They are both studying in Ann Arbor, Michigan. Amy, from New York, is asking Yoko, a Japanese woman, about her trip to Michigan and her first impression of the airport and Ann Arbor.

Listen to the conversation and look at the information on the plane ticket and the taxi receipt. On the Yoko's First Day worksheet, write down as much as you can about Yoko's first day in the United States.

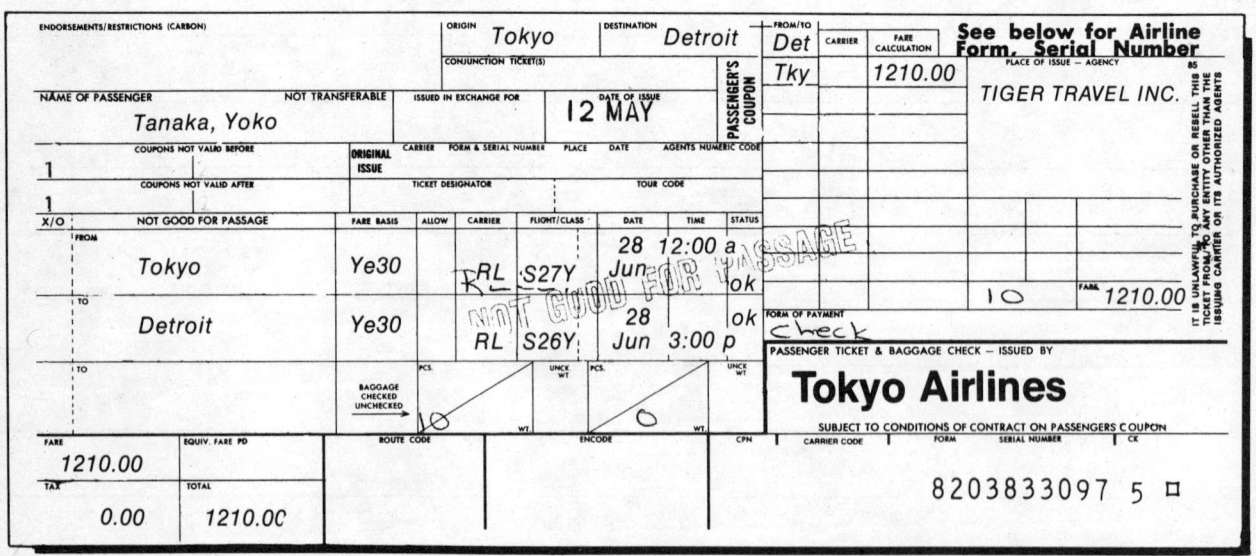

Yoko's First Day

Arrival (day, time, etc.)	1 year ago
Airline	
Travel time	
At the airport	
Travel to Ann Arbor	
First night	
Other information	

- Review the information from the worksheet and then complete the following story about Yoko's first day in the United States.

My friend, Yoko, _____ to Michigan about _____ year ago. She _____ on Tokyo airlines. It took _____ hours to travel from _____ to _____. Nobody _____ at the airport to meet _____. She _____ a taxi to Ann Arbor. It _____ $24.

The first night in Ann Arbor she _____ at a hotel. When she arrived in Ann Arbor, she didn't

_____

44 **Lesson 12**

Ann Arbor

Student Notes:

- Work with two of your classmates. Ask your partners questions about their first day in the United States or their first day in a new country or city. Complete the following chart.

	Classmate No. 1	Classmate No. 2
Name		
Arrival (day, time, etc.)		
Airline(s)		
Travel time		
At the airport		
Travel from airport		
First night		
Other information (feelings, impressions, etc.)		

Lesson 12

- Write a short composition about the first day in the United States of one of your partners. Be sure to include the person's impressions and feelings.

  _____
  _____
  _____
  _____
  _____
  _____
  _____
  _____
  _____

- Write down five questions you asked your partners about their first day in the United States.

  1. When _____ the United States?
  2. What airline(s) _____?
  3. How long _____?
  4. _____?
  5. _____?

Student Notes:

- Fill in the blanks with the correct past tense form.

be	*was, were*	have	_____
buy	*bought*	make	_____
come	_____	read	_____
cost	_____	see	_____
do	_____	sit	_____
drink	_____	speak	_____
drive	_____	take	_____
eat	_____	think	_____
get	_____	understand	_____
go	_____	write	_____

Lesson 13   Alibi

📼 A police officer is interviewing two suspects in a robbery that took place on Monday evening.

1. Listen to the interview* and write down the suspect's alibi (where s/he was, what s/he was doing, etc.). The teacher will assign half the class to Tape A (Alan Carter) and the other half to Tape B (Fran Greer).

2. When you have written down all the information from your tape, check your notes with the other students in your group.

3. Exchange information with a partner from the other group and write down the alibi for that suspect. Then, using the clues on page 49, decide who you think committed the crime.

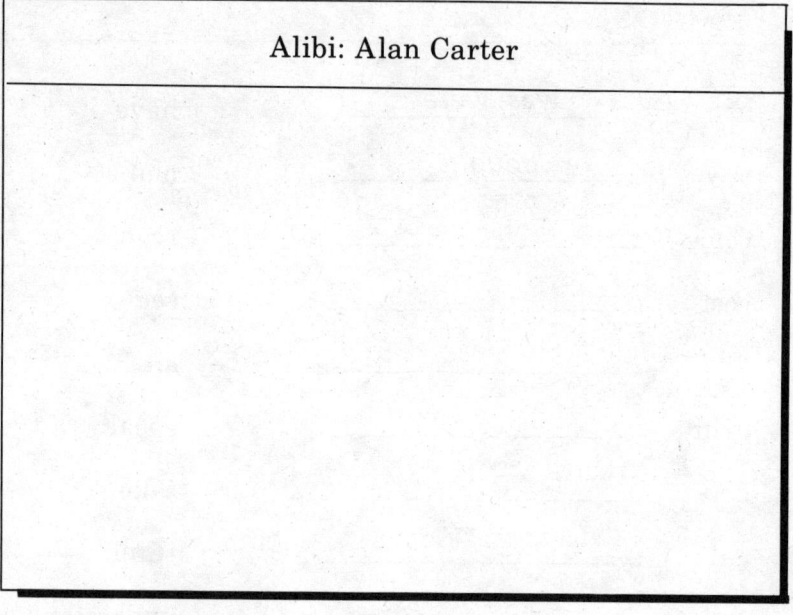

Alibi: Alan Carter

Alibi: Fran Greer

---

*Based on "Alibi" in *Discussions That Work* by Penny Ur, pp. 58–60.
© Cambridge University Press 1981.

Lesson 13   49

VILLAGE THEATER

$2.50 Monday through Friday
Shows starting before 6:00
Sat. and Sun. first show only

1209 Main Street   579-0146

My Bodyguard
10:00, 12:00, 2:30, 4:30, 7:00, 9:00
The Color Purple
10:10, 12:30, 2:45, 5:00, 7:30, 9:30
Bliss
10:30, 12:30, 3:00, 5:15, 7:15, 9:15
Room with a View
12:15, 2:45, 5:00, 7:15, 9:30

FOX THEATER

1104 Nile Road   578-1149

Pretty in Pink
12:00, 2:15, 4:30, 7:00, 9:45
Official Story
12:00, 2:30, 4:45, 7:00, 9:45
The Gods Must Be Crazy
12:00, 2:15, 4:45, 7:00, 9:45

Imperial Restaurant

CHINESE AND AMERICAN FOOD

COCKTAILS
LUNCHEON SPECIALS

Tues. to Thurs., 11:30–9:30
Fri., Sat., and Sun., 11:00–10:30
Closed Monday
Carry-out Service
Bar Open til 2:00
110 South Seventh Street
549-0912

PIZZA PALACE

ITALIAN RESTAURANT

GOOD FOOD!
PIZZA   PASTA
SUBMARINE SANDWICHES
Eat in or Carry out
548-1172
509 Fourth Avenue
Downtown

Gym Building Hours

M–F	7 a.m.–9 p.m.
Sa	9 a.m.–9 p.m.
Su	noon–9 p.m.

- Who do you think has a weak alibi? Why? Give four reasons.

Name: _____
1. _____
2. _____
3. _____
4. _____

- Now, write down five questions that the policeman asked about the restaurant, the movie, and the gym.

1. _____ ?
2. _____ ?
3. _____ ?
4. _____ ?
5. _____ ?

- Last night a robbery took place just outside of your town. The police think that the robbery took place between 7:00 P.M. and 10:00 P.M. You and your partner(s) are possible *suspects*. The police think you and your partner(s) may have committed the crime.

    Your lawyer has advised your group to create an *alibi* for every minute between 7:00 and 10:00. Write notes on where you were, what you were doing, who you were with, and any details such as how much money you spent, how you went from one place to another, etc. The *jury* will question you and your partner(s) separately to find out if you have *the same alibi*.

    If your alibi is broken—that is, if you and your partner(s) do not agree on something—you may be found *guilty*.

Reminder—you will probably be asked some of the following questions:

a. Where were you at 7:00?
b. Who was with you?
c. Did you eat dinner? What did you order? How much did it cost?
d. What were you wearing?

You must answer all questions. You cannot say, "I don't know" or "I don't remember."

Alibi Notes:

7:00–8:00 P.M.

8:00–9:00 P.M.

9:00–10:00 P.M.

- Complete the following dialogue between a policeman and a suspect:

Q: Where ___were___ you at 7:00 last night?

A: Last night I _____ to a movie.

Q: What movie did you _____?

A: E.T.

Q: How _____ you get to the movie?

A: I _____ a bus.

Q: How much _____ the movie ticket _____?

A: About $3.50.

Q: What time did the film _____?

A: At about 9:00.

Q: Then, what did you _____?

A: I _____ a newspaper at the drugstore.

Q: _____ you go home after that?

A: No, I _____. I _____ my homework at the library and then went home.

Student Notes:

Lesson 14 How Good Is Your Geography?

- Work in small groups. Decide whether these statements are *true* (**T**) or *false* (**F**) and circle the correct answer. If statements are *false*, tell why.

1. There are fifty states in the United States. T F
2. The biggest state in the United States is Texas. T F
3. Korea is an island. T F
4. The biggest country in Central America is El Salvador. T F
5. The capital of Saudi Arabia is Mecca. T F
6. Las Vegas is in California. T F
7. The Canary Islands belong to Spain. T F
8. The United States is smaller than Canada. T F
9. The highest mountain in the world is Mount McKinley. T F
10. Washington, D.C. (District of Columbia), is a state. T F
11. Angel Falls is located in Mexico. T F
12. Argentina is the largest South American country. T F
13. Thailand borders on Vietnam. T F
14. There are four Great Lakes—Lake Superior, Lake Ontario, Lake Erie, and Lake Huron. T F
15. The longest river in the world is the Amazon. T F
16. Czechoslovakia is north of Poland. T F

Lesson 14   53

17. Niagara Falls belongs to the United States and Canada.   T F

18. The Sudan is the largest country in Africa.   T F

19. Japan's closest neighbor is China.   T F

20. The Pyrenees Mountains divide France and Italy.   T F

21. Saudi Arabia is in Africa.   T F

22. India has the largest population in the world.   T F

23. Equador, Kenya, Indonesia and Australia are on the equator.   T F

Lesson 14

Can you make up two "tricky" geography statements for your classmates?

24. _____ T   F

25. _____ T   F

- Return to five of the statements you have circled **F** and rewrite them so that they are true.

1. _____

2. _____

3. _____

4. _____

5. _____

Student Notes:

Lesson 14   55

- This is a map of the United States. The names of ten (10) states are missing from the map. Ask your teacher questions to find out the names of the missing states. Write the names of the states on the map.

- Read the information about the United States and then complete the information sheet on page 57.

The United States

The United States is located in North America between the Atlantic Ocean to the east and the Pacific Ocean to the west. Its closest neighbors are Canada to the north and Mexico to the south. The United States is the second largest country in the Western Hemisphere, with a land area of 3,540,938 square miles (9,170,989 square kilometers).

According to the 1980 census, the population of the United States is 226,545,805. The capital, Washington, D.C., which is located on the East Coast between Maryland and Virginia, was chosen by George Washington, the first president.

The main commercial center of the United States is New York City, located in the southeast corner of New York State. It has a population of 7,072,000 inhabitants, making it the largest city in the country. Sprawling Los Angeles, found in the southwest section of California, is the second largest city with a population of 2,967,000.

There are now fifty states in the United States. The two newest states, Alaska and Hawaii, joined the Union in 1959, at which time Alaska replaced Texas as the largest state. Mount McKinley, the highest mountain in the country, is located in the south central section of Alaska. It is 20,320 feet (6,194 meters) high.

The Mississippi River, which runs along the eastern borders of Minnesota, Iowa, Missouri, Arkansas, and Louisiana, is the longest river in the United States. It flows 2,348 miles (3,757 kilometers) from the Rocky Mountains to the Gulf of Mexico. Lake Superior is the biggest lake. It is located in the northernmost section of Michigan, bordering on Canada.

The United States

Population:

Capital:

Largest city (by population):

   population:

Second largest city (by population):

   population:

Largest state (by area):

Second largest state (by area):

Highest mountain:

   height:

Longest river:

   length:

Largest lake:

- Write the following names in the correct location on the map of the United States.

1. Washington, D.C.
2. New York City
3. Los Angeles
4. Mount McKinley
5. Mississippi River
6. Lake Superior

Lesson 14

- Interview your partner and complete the following information sheet about your partner's country.

> Country:
>
> Location:
>
> Population:
>
> Capital:
>
> Most important city:
>
>   population:
>
> Second most important city:
>
>   population:
>
> Highest mountain(s):
>
> Longest river:
>
> Largest lake:
>
> Largest desert:
>
> Other interesting features:

- Have your partner draw a map of her/his country and then, with your partner, add the geographical features to the map.

Lesson 15 Choosing a City

📼 Linda has been offered a new job with the Kizner Corporation. She can choose to work in an office in Philadelphia, Pennsylvania, or one in Austin, Texas. She has a friend living in Philadelphia and another one living in Austin. She is calling them to get some information before she decides in which city she would prefer to live and work.

1. Listen to the telephone conversation and write down the information on the worksheet on page 61. The teacher will assign half the class to Tape A (Philadelphia) and the other half to Tape B (Austin).

2. When you have written down the information from your tape, check your answers with the other students in your group.

3. Exchange information with a partner from the other group and write down his/her answers on the appropriate part of the worksheet.

Philadelphia

Lesson 15   61

	Philadelphia	Austin
Attractive?	yes OK no	yes OK no
Population:		
Rent for a small apartment:		
Transportation:	good satisfactory bad	good satisfactory bad
	expensive average cheap	expensive average cheap
Number of restaurants:		
Museums:		
Places to ski:		
Pollution:		
Crime:	high a little high low	high a little high low

Austin

Lesson 15

- With your partner, use the information that you have found to compare Philadelphia, Pennsylvania, to Austin, Texas. Then, working individually, write down a comparative statement about the following items. When you have finished, check your statements with your partner.

Attractiveness: *Philadelphia is not as attractive as Austin. [or] Austin is more attractive than Philadelphia.*

Population: _____

Rent for a one-bedroom apartment: _____

Transportation: _____

Number of restaurants: _____

Museums: _____

Places to ski: _____

Pollution: _____

Crime: _____

Student Notes:

- Compare your partner's city with your own. Ask your partner questions to find out the necessary information to complete the worksheet. If you and your partner live in the same city, compare your city with another city in your country.

	Your City	Your Partner's City or Another City
Attractiveness:		
trees:		
parks:		
mountains:		
Population:		
Rent for a small apartment:		
Transportation:		
good or bad?		
cheap or expensive?		
Restaurants:		
Places to		
ski:		
dance:		
Pollution:		
Crime:		
Weather:		

- Write a composition telling about your partner's city and how it is different from your own. Or, compare your city to another city in your country.

Student Notes:

Lesson 16   Apartments for Rent

📼 John has accepted a job in Toledo. He wants to rent an apartment. He calls to find out information about an apartment for rent.

1. Listen to the conversation and write down the information on the information sheet. The teacher will assign half the class to Tape A (first apartment) and the other half to Tape B (second apartment).

2. When you have written down the information from your tape, check your answers with the other students in your group.

3. Exchange information with a partner from the other group. Write down your partner's information.

	First Apartment	Second Apartment	Third Apartment
Distance from downtown:			5 minutes
Size:			large
Number of bedrooms:			1
Dining room?			no
Furnished?			newly painted, but unfurnished
Rent:			$400.00
Noise?			not much
Kitchen:			very nice!
size:			large
refrigerator?			yes
dishwasher?			no
Fireplace?			yes

Lesson 16

- Compare the three apartments. Fill in the blanks with the correct word or words.

Distance from campus:

The third apartment is ___the closest___ to downtown and the first apartment is _____ from downtown.

Size:

The second apartment is _____ the first one.

Number of bedrooms:

_____ of the apartments has more than one bedroom.

Dining room:

The first apartment _____ a dining room, but the other two _____ .

Furnished:

The furniture in the first apartment is _____ the furniture in the second apartment; and the third apartment _____ have _____ furniture.

Rent:

The third apartment is _____ expensive.

Noise:

_____ of the apartments is noisy; the third apartment is not _____ quiet _____ the other two.

Kitchen:

The third apartment has the _____ kitchen.

_____ apartments have refrigerators, but the second apartment also _____ .

Lesson 16   67

Fireplace:

_____ has a fireplace, but

the other two _____ .

- Now, ask your partner which apartment s/he would rent and why. Write a paragraph summarizing your partner's answers.

_____
_____
_____
_____
_____

- In the tape, what questions did the person looking for an apartment ask?

1. Near/far from downtown: _____
   _____?

2. Size: _____
   _____?

3. Number of bedrooms: _____
   _____?

4. Furnished: _____
   _____?

5. Rent: _____
   _____?

6. Noise: _____
   _____?

7. Kitchen: _____
   _____?

- Interview your partner. Find out what the advantages and disadvantages of his/her house, apartment, or dormitory room are. Write a short composition using this information.

_____

_____

_____

_____

_____

_____

_____

Student Notes:

Lesson 17   Advertisements

- Part One: Finding an Inexpensive Wedding Dress

Sheila is getting married this winter. She wants to buy a wedding gown but doesn't have enough money to buy a new one. So she has decided to look for a used one. She has about $70 to spend. She is 5'7" (1.7 meters) and generally wears size 7 or 9.

Can you and your partner(s) help her find a wedding gown? Read the following advertisements and decide which ads she should respond to.

© José Sánchez H., 1986

Student Notes:

1. WEDDING GOWN AND TRAIN — Lace, size 9, $110, call 424-0909.
2. WEDDING GOWN AND VEIL — Size 5, chantilly lace, short sleeves, $65, call 325-6900.
3. WEDDING DRESS — Simple but very beautiful summer gown with Venice lace, size 18, $85, 434-6789.
4. WEDDING GOWN — Ivory, size 7, $77. 665-4321.
5. WEDDING GOWN — Satin and lace, short sleeves, size 7, $58, call 767-0978.
6. WEDDING GOWN AND VEIL — Satin bridal gown with long sleeves. Size 7. $75 or best offer, 355-5821.

Lesson 17

- Part Two: Finding an Apartment

Carla and Ryan are looking for an apartment. They need a two-bedroom apartment because they are expecting their first child in two months. They don't have very much money because they are both in school. Ryan works part-time at a hotel and Carla works part-time at the university library. They would like to move next month, if possible.

Can you and your partner(s) help Carla and Ryan find an apartment? Which of the following ads should they respond to?

Student Notes:

1. CAMPUS AREA — 1-bedroom apartment, ideal for graduate student or professional couple, 584-1522.

2. FURNISHED CONDO — 2 bedrooms. All appliances, air, garage, fireplace, quiet. Ideal for professional or grad students. No kids or pets. Call 793-0011.

3. ATTRACTIVE — Available in 2 months, 2-bedroom furnished apartments in brick building. Close to campus and downtown. AC and laundry. Call 953-8762.

4. 2-BEDROOM TOWNHOUSE — Georgetown area. 1½ baths, full basement, central air, carpeted with fireplace, $560. For appointment 981-3912.

5. TWO-BEDROOM APT. — Available immediately. Across from football stadium on Main. $380/mo. 966-8700.

6. TREE-LINED, WESTSIDE — Newly remodeled, 3 bedrooms, full basement with laundry, large yard with garden, $490. Call 556-5649 persistently.

- Complete each paragraph by filling in the blanks with a word or phrase.

Sheila can't buy the first wedding dress because it is too _____. The second dress isn't _____ enough and it has short sleeves—_____ cold for December. The third dress is _____, _____ and _____. The fourth dress is the right _____ and just a little _____. The next to the last dress is the _____ and the right price, _____ it has short sleeves. The last dress has long sleeves, is big _____, and she can probably get it for $70.

Carla and Ryan can't take the first apartment because it is _____. The second apartment is _____ but no children are allowed. The third isn't available soon _____. The fourth is _____. The last two look good except the last one is a little _____ and a little _____ expensive.

- Write an advertisement for your house or apartment or something you own. Use some abbreviations, e.g., apartment = apt.

_____

_____

_____

_____

Lesson 18   The English Language Academy

▭ There is a new director at the English Language Academy, a school that teaches English to foreign students. She wants to get information from the students about what they like and don't like about the school. She is interviewing the class president, Daniel.

1. Listen and find out which areas the students think are problem areas.

2. If there is no problem, make a check mark in the column marked *No Problem*. If there is a problem, write down what it is in the column marked *Problem*. Be ready to tell what the problem is.

	No Problem	Problem
Social activities		
parties:		
trips:		
Tuition:		
Classes		
hours per week:		
homework:		
Classrooms		
size:		
blackboards:		
temperature:		
Number of students per class:		
Lounge		
size:		
furniture:		

- What are the problems that Daniel, the class president, mentioned to the director? Fill in the blanks with the correct word or words.

1. There are _____ parties, but there aren't _____ trips.

2. The tuition is _____ high.

3. The students think they have _____ homework. They don't have enough time to speak with Americans.

4. There is _____ classroom space, but there aren't _____ blackboards.

5. The temperature is _____ in the winter.

6. The beginning classes usually have _____ students.

7. The lounge is big _____ and the students think there's _____ furniture.

Student Notes:

- In your group, decide what the problem areas at *your school* are. If your group thinks there is a problem, put a check mark in the appropriate column. Be ready to tell what the problem is.

	No Problem	Problem
Social activities		
parties:		
trips:		
Tuition:		
Classes		
hours per week:		
homework:		
Classrooms		
size:		
blackboards:		
temperature:		
Number of students per class:		
Lounge		
size:		
furniture:		
Other:		
_____		
_____		

Lesson 18 75

- In what areas did you think there were problems? Explain the problems.

  _____
  _____
  _____
  _____
  _____
  _____

In what areas did you think there were no problems?

  _____
  _____
  _____
  _____
  _____

© José Sánchez H., 1986

Lesson 19　　　Exploring the Universe

📼 A teacher is giving a series of lectures on the solar system to his science class students.

　1. Read the introduction silently as your teacher reads it out loud.

　2. Listen to one of the lectures on the solar system. The teacher will assign half the class to listen to Tape A (Lecture I) and the other half to listen to Tape B (Lecture II). Write down the information on the chart for that lecture (see pages 78 and 79).

　3. When you have written down the information from your tape, check your answers with the other students in your group.

　4. Then, exchange information with a partner from the other group and write down the information on the chart for the other lecture.

Introduction

Today we will begin our lecture series on the universe and solar system. Do you know how many planets there are? Do you know which planet is closest to the Earth or which one is farthest from the Earth? Which planet is the largest or which one shines the brightest in the sky?

There will be two lectures. Lecture I will be about the planets closest to the sun and Lecture II will be about the planets farthest from the sun.

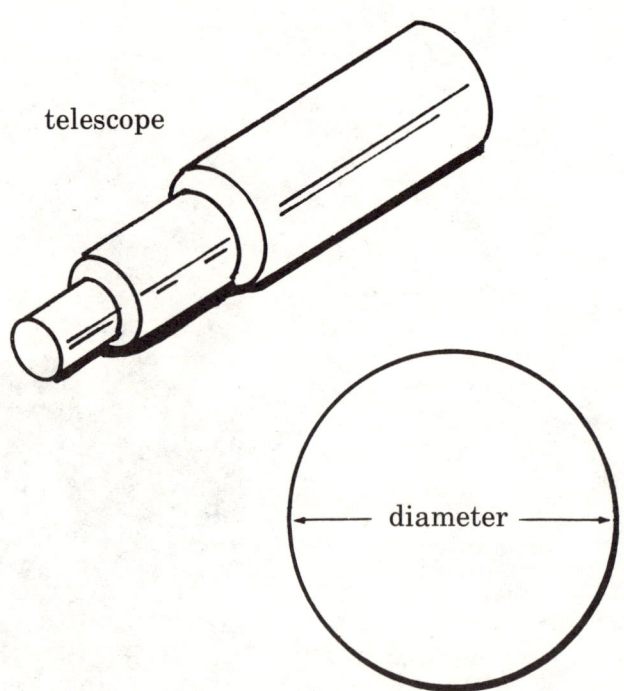

Lecture I

Planet	Distance from Sun	Distance from Earth	Size	Moons	Other Information (color, atmosphere, temperature, etc.)
Mercury					
Venus					
Mars					
Jupiter					

Student Notes:

Lecture II

Planet	Distance from Sun	Distance from Earth	Size	Moons	Other Information (color, atmosphere, temperature, etc.)
Saturn					
Uranus					
Neptune					
Pluto					

Student Notes:

Lesson 19

● **Astronomy Quiz**

Using the information from both lectures on the planets, decide if these statements are true (**T**) or false (**F**).

1. Mars is the smallest planet. T F
2. Uranus is smaller than Earth. T F
3. Four planets are smaller than Earth. T F
4. Jupiter is the largest planet. T F
5. Uranus is the second largest planet. T F
6. Saturn has the most moons. T F
7. Only two planets have no moons. T F
8. Mercury is the planet nearest to Earth. T F
9. Mars is hotter than Earth. T F
10. Pluto is always the farthest from Earth. T F

When you have completed the quiz, return to the items you have circled **F** and write the correct answer.

_____

_____

_____

_____

_____

_____

Lesson 19 81

- In your group or with the whole class, discuss the following questions and write down your answers.

1. Why do people study astronomy? Why do people want to know about planets, stars, the sun, moons, etc.?

2. How will the following be different in the year 2500?

   Transportation: _____
   _____
   _____

   Food: _____
   _____
   _____

   Marriage: _____
   _____
   _____

   Clothing: _____
   _____
   _____

   Music: _____
   _____
   _____

Student Notes:

Lesson 20 Choosing a University

- Read the following paragraph about the University of Miami. Write down the information on the information sheet. Then, find out about your partner's university and complete the Eastern Michigan University section of the information sheet.

Student Notes:

University of Miami

The University of Miami is located in the suburban area of Coral Gables, Florida. This private university was founded in 1925 and now has over 13,000 students. The 260-acre campus includes 119 buildings and a library of 1,400,000 volumes. Miami offers a variety of courses in such fields as business administration, physical education, journalism, nursing, marine science, architecture, engineering, economics, and mathematics. The ratio of students to professors is 17:1. Tuition at Miami is $6,550 a year. Financial aid is available in the form of scholarships, loans, and work study. Students can live in dormitories and eat in campus dining halls. Room and board per year is $2,800. Apartments for married students are available. Fourteen percent of all the students are from foreign countries. A foreign student must score 550 on the TOEFL to be admitted. No college entrance exam is required for foreign students. The application fee is $30.*

*Information taken from *Barron's Profiles of American Colleges* (Woodbury, N.Y.: Barron's Educational Series, 1984).

Lesson 20 83

	University of Miami	Eastern Michigan University
State or private:		
Year founded:		
Number of students:		
Size of campus:		
Tuition per year:		
Financial aid:		
Cost of room and board per semester:		
Married student housing:		
Percentage of foreign students:		
TOEFL or Michigan Test score needed:		
College entrance exam for foreign students:		
Application fee:		

What other information would you like to know about a university?

1. _____
2. _____
3. _____

Lesson 20

- Read the following paragraph about Eastern Michigan University. Write down the information on the information sheet. Then, find out about your partner's university and complete the University of Miami section of the information sheet.

Student Notes:

Eastern Michigan University

Eastern Michigan University is located in Ypsilanti, Michigan, 35 miles from Detroit. This state university was founded in 1849 and now has almost 19,000 students. The 460-acre campus includes 111 buildings and a library of 551,000 volumes. Eastern offers courses in a variety of fields including business administration, special education, art, nursing, chemistry, computer science, social work, criminology, and economics. The ratio of students to professors is 20 to 1. Tuition at Eastern is $1,444 a year for Michigan residents and $3,431 a year for nonresidents. Financial aid is available in the form of work study, scholarships, and loans. Room and board per year is $2,398. Married student housing is available. Five percent of all full-time students are from foreign countries. A foreign student must score 500 on the TOEFL or 80 on the Michigan Test. No college entrance exam is required for foreign students. There is no application fee.*

*Information taken from *Barron's Profiles of American Colleges* (Woodbury, N.Y.: Barron's Educational Series, 1984).

Lesson 20 85

	Eastern Michigan University	University of Miami
State or private:		
Year founded:		
Number of students:		
Size of campus:		
Tuition per year:		
Financial aid:		
Cost of room and board per semester:		
Married student housing:		
Percentage of foreign students:		
TOEFL or Michigan Test score needed:		
College entrance exam for foreign students:		
Application fee:		

What other information would you like to know about a university?

1. _____

2. _____

3. _____

Lesson 20

- Write sentences comparing the two universities. One comparison has already been written.

1. *Both universities have financial aid for students.*
2. _____
3. _____
4. _____
5. _____
6. _____
7. _____

Which university would you choose? Why?

_____
_____
_____
_____
_____
_____

Lesson 21   Traffic Laws

- In small groups, discuss what each of the following expressions or signs means.

    1. Traffic

    2. Traffic light

    3. Blinking traffic light

    4. Traffic laws

    5. Seat belts

    6. Driver's license

    7. License plates

    8. Parking ticket

    9. Car insurance

    10.

    11. PAY TOLL AHEAD

    12. Highways

Lesson 21

- With your partner, complete the following sentences by filling in the blanks. There may be more than one correct answer.

1. A blinking red light means you _____ stop.

2. A [DO NOT ENTER] means you _____ go through.

3. On highways in the United States, you _____ pass on the left, not on the right.

4. A [no U-turn] sign means you _____ make a U-turn.

5. A [WALK] sign means you _____ walk across the street.

6. A [YIELD] sign means you _____ slow down.

7. A [SPEED LIMIT 55 MINIMUM 45] sign means you _____ go slower than 45 miles per hour.

8. When you see an ambulance, you _____ stop your car.

9. In most of the states in the United States, you _____ make a right turn on a red light.

10. You _____ stop at a blinking yellow light but you _____ slow down.

Student Notes:

- What is your opinion about the following statements? What is your partner's opinion? Do you agree or disagree? Complete the Opinion Survey for yourself, then find out from your partner what s/he thinks and complete her/his part of the survey.

Opinion Survey	You		Your Partner	
	Yes	No	Yes	No
1. Everybody should wear seatbelts.				
2. Only children should wear seatbelts.				
3. Drunk drivers should go to jail and lose their license.				
4. Drivers should not have TVs in the front seat.				
5. People should not drive until they are 21.				
6. Bike riders should ride in the streets, not on the sidewalks.				
7. Every car owner should have insurance.				
8. People over 80 years old should not drive.				
9. The speed limit should be higher than 55 m.p.h. (U.S. speed limit is 55 m.p.h.)				
10. Policemen should take bribes, especially if they receive a low salary.				

- How many in your class agree with the Opinion Survey statements? Write down the number who agree and disagree for each statement. Then compare your class with a class of fifteen students at the American Language Academy and complete the summary statements.

Opinion Survey Results	Class at ALA Yes	Class at ALA No	Your Class Yes	Your Class No
1. Everybody should wear seatbelts.	8	7		
2. Only children should wear seatbelts.	7	8		
3. Drunk drivers should go to jail and lose their license.	14	1		
4. Drivers should not have TVs in the front seat.	13	2		
5. People should not drive until they are 21.	4	11		
6. Bike riders should ride in the streets, not on the sidewalks.	9	6		
7. Every car owner should have insurance.	5	10		
8. People over 80 years old should not drive.	4	11		
9. The speed limit should be higher than 55 m.p.h. (U.S. speed limit is 55 m.p.h.)	15	0		
10. Policemen should take bribes, especially if they receive a low salary.	0	15		

Summary statements:

Most of the ALA students agree that drivers should not have TVs in their front seat. In my class, _____

_____

Only a few of the ALA students agree that people over 80 years old should not drive. In my class, _____

_____

_____ of the ALA students agree that policemen should take bribes. In my class, _____

_____

Everybody in the ALA agrees that _____

_____ .

In my class, _____

_____

At the ALA, _____

_____

_____

_____

Student Notes:

Lesson 22   Planning a Weekend

📼 Two friends are going to New York City next Saturday and Sunday. They want to plan their weekend carefully. Listen to the tape and check off the activities they choose.

	Yes	No
Saturday:		
Sightseeing along Fifth Avenue	☐	☐
Rockefeller Center	☐	☐
Statue of Liberty	☐	☐
Afternoon show	☐	☐
Evening show	☐	☐
Long Day's Journey into Night	☐	☐
Cats	☐	☐
Arsenic and Old Lace	☐	☐
Dinner in the hotel	☐	☐
Dinner at the theater district	☐	☐
Sunday:		
Botanical garden	☐	☐
Concert	☐	☐
Bronx Zoo	☐	☐
Metropolitan Museum of Art	☐	☐
Museum of Modern Art	☐	☐
Train station at 6:30	☐	☐

First, fill in each blank with one of the following modals. Discuss your answers with your partner. Then, listen to the tape again and compare your choices with those on the tape.

Student Notes:

Modals: **should, could, have to, would rather ('d rather)**

1. What _____ we do first?

2. We _____ check in at our hotel.

3. We _____ go sightseeing along Fifth Avenue.

4. What show _____ we go to see?

5. Or, we _____ go to the zoo.

6. I _____ go to the museums, even if it doesn't rain.

7. What time do we _____ be at the train station on Sunday?

8. I suppose we _____ be at the station by 7:30.

- What would you and your partner like to do on a weekend in New York? Choose from the following activities and plan your weekend. Make a list of the things you and your partner would like to do. Add some of your own ideas.

Music

New York City Opera, New York State Theatre, *Kismet*, 8 P.M.

Mostly Mozart Festival Orchestra, Avery Fisher Hall, 8 P.M., $15, $13, $8

New York Shakespeare Festival, Central Park, *Twelfth Night*, free performance, 8 P.M., daily except Monday

Music Festival on the Pier, Twelfth Ave. and 45th St., Chick Corea's Electric Band, etc., 7:30 P.M.

Sports

Baseball: N.Y. Mets at Shea Stadium; N.Y. Yankees at Yankee Stadium; evening, 7:35, day, 1:35, check schedule for home games

Racing: Belmont, Long Island, daily at 1:00 P.M.

Activities/Museums

New York Aquarium, Coney Island, Brooklyn, open 10 A.M. daily, admission $3.75

Walking tour, Greenwich Village, sponsored by the Museum of the City of New York, 1:30 Sunday

Museum of Modern Art, 53rd St., open daily 11 to 6 except Wednesday, Thursday until 9

American Museum of Natural History, Central Park West at 79th St., open daily, free admission after 5

Hayden Planetarium, 81st and Central Park West, open daily, $3.25

Bronx Zoo (New York Zoological Park) and New York Botanical Garden, Fordham Rd. and Southern Blvd.

Rockefeller Center, Fifth Ave. and 50th St., hour-long tours leave the RCA Building Mon.–Sat.

United Nations Headquarters, First Ave. between 42nd and 48th St., open daily 9:00–4:45, adults $3, college and high school students $1.75, junior high and elementary students $1.25

Theater

Cats, Winter Garden Theatre, Mon.–Sat., 8 P.M., $45, $37.50, $30; Wed., 2 P.M., $40, $32.50, $25

The Search for Signs of Intelligent Life in the Universe, Lily Tomlin, Plymouth Theatre, Tues.–Thurs. and Sat., 8 P.M.; Fri., 7 P.M.

Your Weekend

Saturday:

Sunday:

Lesson 22

- What did you or your partner(s) say or ask about the following? Try to use different forms, e.g., *We could _____, I'd rather not _____, Should we _____?*, etc.

Mostly Mozart Festival: *Would you like to go to the Festival?*

Walking tour: _____

Yankees baseball game: _____

United Nations: _____

Cats: _____

Music Festival on the Pier: _____

New York Aquarium: _____

Bronx Zoo: _____

- Now, complete the following letter to a friend. Tell your friend about your weekend and suggest that your friend meet you and your partner in New York.

_____

Dear _____ ,

   This weekend _____ [partner's name] and I are going to New York. We _____ you to join us in New York. Our train arrives at 9:30. _____ you meet us at _____ on Saturday at about 10:30? Then, we _____

_____

Later, would you like to _____ ?

On Sunday, _____ .

After that, would you rather _____ or _____ ? Then we _____ .

Our train leaves New York on Sunday at 9:35 P.M., so we _____ at the train station by about 8:35 P.M. We're looking forward to seeing you in New York.

                                   Your friend,

                                   _____

Lesson 23   Hiring an E.S.L. Teacher

▭ The Adult Education Program needs a new teacher for next semester. The director has called two people who are interested in the position (job).

   1. Listen to the phone conversation and write down the information on the resume form. The teacher will assign half the class to Tape A (Robin Wilson) and the other half to Tape B (Suzanne Jones).

   2. When you have written down the information from your tape, check your answers with the other students in your group.

   3. Exchange information with a partner from the other group and complete the resume form.

Resume Form

	Robin Wilson	Suzanne Jones
Name:		
Degree(s):		
Teaching experience		
present:		
past:		
Travel:		
Languages:		
Other information:		

- Study each resume carefully and decide with your partner who should get the job—Robin Wilson or Suzanne Jones. Write down who you think should get the job and the reasons why. Be specific about why your choice is better.

_____ should get the position for the following reasons:

_____

_____

_____

_____

_____

_____

_____

_____

Student Notes:

Lesson 23

- Complete the following paragraphs by putting the correct word or words in the blanks.

Suzanne Jones _____ teaching English _____ foreign students in Arizona. She has _____ there for _____ years. She also _____ literature in Greece for two years. She _____ traveled to the Middle East and speaks fluent Greek and some _____.

She received her _____ degree ten years _____ from the University of Southern California. She could begin teaching in June or September.

Robin Wilson _____ teaching English to foreign students in Miami. She has _____ there _____ two years. Three years ago she _____ _____ at a community college in Chicago. She _____ never _____ in a foreign country, but she _____ to Colombia, Mexico, and Japan. She speaks _____.

She _____ her _____ degree _____ ago from _____. She could begin teaching _____.

- Interview a professional in your class to find out the following information. Work in small groups or as a class.

Name:

Experience

  present:

  past:

Education:

Travel:

Language(s):

Publications:

_____ date: _____

_____ date: _____

Medical history (list serious illnesses only):

_____ date: _____

_____ date: _____

Comments:

Lesson 23

- Review the information you have written down and write a short composition about your classmate's professional history.

My classmate is _____

_____

_____

_____

_____

Lesson 24 Questionnaire

- Interview the people in your class. Walk around the room and ask questions to complete the questionnaire.

1. Who in your class has studied English the longest?

   Name: _____

   How long? _____

2. Who in your class speaks another foreign language besides English?

   Name: _____

   Language: _____

3. Who in your class has had good luck or bad luck this year?

   Name: _____

   What happened? _____

4. Who in your class has been married for over 5 years?

   Name: _____

   How long? _____

5. Who in your class has never driven a car?

   Name: _____

6. Who in your class can fly a plane?

   Name: _____

7. How many people in your class have been to Disney World?

   Number: _____

8. Who in your class will take a trip soon?

   Name: _____

   Where? _____

9. Who in your class has had an operation?

   Name: _____

   What kind? _____

10. Who in your class has ever found anything valuable?

    Name: _____

    What? _____

11. Who has traveled the farthest to study English?

    Name: _____

12. Who hasn't been absent from class yet this semester?

    Name: _____

Student Notes:

Fill in the blanks with the correct form of the past tense and the past participle.

be	was, were	been	find	_____	_____	ride	_____	_____
begin	_____	_____	fly	_____	_____	send	_____	_____
break	_____	_____	get	_____	_____	sit	_____	_____
bring	_____	_____	give	_____	_____	spend	_____	_____
buy	_____	_____	go	_____	_____	speak	_____	_____
catch	_____	_____	have	_____	_____	take	_____	_____
come	_____	_____	hear	_____	_____	teach	_____	_____
cost	_____	_____	know	_____	_____	think	_____	_____
cut	_____	_____	make	_____	_____	throw	_____	_____
drink	_____	_____	meet	_____	_____	understand	_____	_____
drive	_____	_____	put	_____	_____	wear	_____	_____
eat	_____	_____	read	_____	_____	write	_____	_____